JOINT LITURGICAL (

A Four Y

Lectionary

VO

JLG 2

The Canterbury Press
Norwich

First published 1990 for the Joint Liturgical Group
by The Canterbury Press Norwich
(a publishing imprint of Hymns Ancient & Modern Limited)
St Mary's Works, St Mary's Plain,
Norwich, Norfolk, NR3 3BH

Reprinted 1992

British Library Cataloguing in Publication Data
A Four year lectionary.
1. Christian church. Public worship
I. Joint Liturgical Group
264

ISBN 1–85311–021–3

Typeset by Cambridge Composing UK Ltd
and printed in Great Britain by
St Edmundsbury Press Ltd, Bury St Edmunds, Suffolk

Foreword

This booklet is a further contribution by the Joint Liturgical Group to the continuing search, in Great Britain and beyond, for a lectionary which is able to serve the differing needs of the Churches. It is a search which we believe is well worth persuing, for it must always be a strengthening of the links between the Churches if, when one congregation meets for worship on a Sunday, they can be aware of the fact their ecumenical neighbours are 'sitting under' the same portions of scripture at their services.

As is pointed out in the Introduction, the JLG is currently contributing to other work towards a common lectionary, but believe that this present piece of work follows a line which has hitherto not been explored, yet has much merit in it.

The original idea for a four-year lectionary of this sort came from Donald McIlhagga, who was at the time one of the URC's representatives on the Group. Since then Raymond George and Neville Clark have given a good deal of time to developing the idea.

The Joint Liturgical Group offers this lectionary to the Churches for their detailed study and careful consideration.

DONALD GRAY
Chairman

1st September 1990

MEMBERS OF THE JOINT LITURGICAL GROUP

Church of England:
The Revd Canon Dr Donald Gray
The Revd M R Vasey

Church of Scotland:
The Revd C Robertson
The Revd A Scobie

The Baptist Church of Great Britain and Ireland:
The Revd N Clark
The Revd P Sheppy

The United Reformed Church:
The Revd Dr Colin Thompson
The Revd Susan Durber

The Scottish Episcopal Church:
The Revd Canon Dr Gianfranco Tellini

The Methodist Church:
The Revd A R George
The Revd Dr G S Wakefield

The Roman Catholic Church:
The Revd P M Gallacher
Dr Donald Withey

The Fellowship of the Churches of Christ:
the Revd E Greer

The Church in Wales:
The Revd D Thomas

Introduction

Two lectionaries for Sundays and other principal days are in widespread use today in the English-speaking world and indeed to some extent beyond it. One is the three-year cycle, either in the form of the current Roman Catholic lectionary or in the modification of the Roman scheme known as *The Common Lectionary* (CL) prepared by the Consultation on Common Texts (CCT), based on the United States of America and Canada. This is widely used in those countries and also in some others. The other is the two-year cycle in *The Calendar and Lectionary* by the Joint Liturgical Group (JLG), ed. Ronald C. D. Jasper (O.U.P., 1967), a body originally based on England and Scotland, and now also on Wales. This lectionary also is used in some other parts of the world. The JLG publication *The Word in Season*, ed. Donald Gray (The Canterbury Press Norwich, 1988), made some comparison of these two systems and considered the possibility of combining their best features.

The English Language Liturgical Consultation (ELLC), wishing to encourage and facilitate the development of an international ecumenical lectionary, has recognised CL as the basis from which work towards this lectionary should be carried forward, and asked CCT for representation on the CCT Task Force which is engaged on the revision of CL. This request was granted, and one of the representatives of ELLC is a member of JLG, which will thus have some 'input' into the final form of CL. It does not seem possible, however, for CL to embody the main distinctive principles of JLG. ELLC has also expressed the hope that the Roman Catholic Church will be engaged as partner and leader in the ongoing process of lectionary evaluation and development.

JLG has now revised its 1967 Lectionary, hereafter called JLG 1; this present book *A Four Year Lectionary*, contains that revision, hereafter called JLG 2.

JLG has decided to recommend to its member-churches the use of either CL or JLG 2 or both. The rest of this introduction deals primarily with JLG 2, though with occasional reference to its relation to CL.

JLG 2 preserves the fundamental principles of JLG 1, but with one important innovation. These fundamental principles are the distinctive calendar of JLG 1, of which the most striking feature was the nine Sundays of preparation for Christmas, and the links between the three lessons each Sunday. The important innovation adopted by JLG 2 is that it covers four years rather than two, and, apart from a few special days, one year is devoted to each of the gospels. This extension to four years meets the objection that too little scripture is covered and that the same passages recur too frequently. Detailed statistics later in this book show that a much fuller and richer diet of scripture is provided. It has thus been possible to introduce a greater element of narrative. The use of one gospel each year is of course derived from the Roman lectionary and CL, which devote one year to each of the synoptic gospels and use John in all three years. By devoting a fourth year to John, JLG 2 adopts this valuable principle and carries it further.

JLG 2 has abandoned the terminology of 'controlling lessons', which sometimes led preachers to think that they must always preach on the controlling lessons and thus led to the neglect of the other lessons. Nevertheless the retention of the JLG calendar means that the lessons for the year still cover in order the whole biblical story from the creation of the world to the heavenly city, and individual narratives can be seen in that context.

Similarly JLG 2 has abandoned the terminology of 'themes', which sometimes led to JLG 1 being unfairly dismissed as 'thematic'. JLG 2 has retained links between the three lessons each Sunday. The links between the Old Testament readings and the New Testament readings, whether epistles or gospels, are not necessarily 'typological', but are more varied and subtle and to some extent theologically more defensible. It cannot be too strongly emphasized that preachers are not expected to discover a 'theme' and then preach on it, perhaps with scant regard to the passages, but to preach on any of the passages; sometimes indeed a preacher may refer to all of them, weaving them all into the sermon, but that is not essential. A preacher may well preach on only one of them; the others, as they are read, will speak for themselves.

Another advantage of JLG 2 is that it represents the balance of scripture better by including more passages about women, such as are contained, for example, in the list suggested in the report of the General Synod of the Church of England, *Making Women Visible.*

In some particular cases JLG 2 prefers comprehensibility to brevity, but overall, as the figures later in this book show, the total number of verses used on any Sunday is almost exactly the same as in JLG 1.

It is sometimes difficult to know where best to begin or end a passage because of the variations between different translations. One version's full stop may be another version's comma. JLG 2 has been guided by the sense of the passages and to some extent by indications of the sense which are offered by the most recent versions. But those using other versions may sometimes need to omit at the beginning a connecting word such as 'And' or 'Therefore' or to make other minor adjustments. It will often be well to indicate who is the speaker.

We now make more detailed comments on the course of the year.

JLG 1 had controlling lessons from the Old Testament for the nine Sundays before Christmas. It is easy to see that Creation, Fall, Abraham and Moses are still there in JLG 2. JLG 1 had Noah after Fall; the gap caused by the almost universal practice of omitting Noah was filled in many churches by moving up Abraham and Moses and inserting The Remnant on the fifth Sunday before Christmas. That Sunday is now observed by Roman Catholics as Christ the King and in accord with this JLG 2 has lessons dealing with kingship. The Sunday could, however, be regarded as dealing chiefly with kingship as an Old Testament topic. Thereafter, JLG 2 follows JLG 1 in moving into the more immediate Advent preparation in terms of Advent hope, Word of God, Forerunner, Annunciation, with the continued recognition of the widespread observance of the third Sunday before Christmas (Advent 2) as Bible Sunday.

Though JLG 1 had lessons for Epiphany, it continued to number the following Sundays as Sundays after Christmas; JLG 2, as is the common practice, numbers them after Epiphany. JLG 1 presupposed a fixed Easter, but JLG 2 provides for the full possible number of Sundays after Epiphany and after Pentecost. The Last Sunday after Pentecost is so described in JLG 2, so that some of the preceding Sundays will in some years be omitted.

The Sundays after Epiphany still include events from the beginning of Christ's ministry, beginning with the Baptism of Christ on Epiphany 1, though on the later Sundays after Epiphany, omitted in some years, the lessons range more widely. These Sundays, unlike the Sundays after Pentecost, still have some links across the years.

The Sundays before Easter, including Lent, continue much as before, and the emphasis on Christ the Teacher on the ninth Sunday before Easter facilitates its observance as Education Sunday. JLG 1 has for the fourth Sunday before Easter (Lent 3) the theme 'The King and the Kingdom: Suffering'. This is indeed one of the aspects of the Gospel passages which in both years deal with the events at Caesarea Philippi, a turning-point in Christ's ministry and a prelude to the Passion. In JLG 2 three years deal with these events; the John year has a passage which, though earlier in Christ's ministry, marks a somewhat similar turning-point in Christ's relations with his disciples. That the Transfiguration follows immediately in the synoptic gospels is a good reason for keeping it on the next Sunday, the third Sunday before Easter (Lent 4), despite the fact that both the Roman and the Common Lectionary, though varying from each other, have it on a different day. These lessons are also appropriate on the Sunday nearest August 6, the traditional date of the Transfiguration in many churches. The John year has a passage which leads up to the events of Holy Week.

The treatment of Palm Sunday and Easter Day is more closely related to traditional observances, as represented in JLG's book *Holy Week Services*, ed. Donald Gray (Revised and expanded edition, SPCK, 1983). The service on Palm Sunday has been separated into two distinct parts, the first dealing with the triumphal entry and the second with the passion. JLG 1 has two sets for Easter, meant respectively for 8 a.m. and mid-morning services. The first has been expanded in JLG 2, so that it may be used either at a vigil or at an early morning service.

Pentecost 1 is still observed as Trinity Sunday. Thereafter JLG 2 begins the semi-continuous reading of Matthew, Mark and John. In the Luke year there is a short semi-continuous series of readings from Acts, beginning indeed at Pentecost, accompanied by Luke passages which are not semi-continuous; and the semi-continuous reading of Luke begins when the Acts passages are concluded.

After Pentecost 1 there are in JLG 2 no longer links across the years (apart from the Last Sunday after Pentecost) such as there were in JLG 1 from Pentecost 7 onwards. But whereas JLG 1 after Pentecost had links between one Sunday and the next only occasionally, as from Pentecost 1 to 5 (Second Year) and from Pentecost 11 to 13, in JLG 2 the semi-continuous reading of a Gospel or of Acts provides a kind of link between each Sunday and the next. Each Sunday, as in JLG 1, still has links between its own three lessons. The importance of these links throughout the year as of the other features of JLG 2 is more fully expounded in the chapter that follows.

Three things have not been done. It remains to be seen whether JLG will eventually do them.

First, JLG never had a table of Psalms, though some churches compiled tables to fit JLG 1. The Psalms should not be neglected.

Secondly, many of the JLG collects in *The Daily Office Revised*, ed. Ronald C. D. Jasper (SPCK, 1978), adopted with modifications by many churches, will no longer be appropriate, especially after Pentecost, and it might be better, at any rate as an interim measure, to use collects of a more general petitionary nature; good examples can be found in current service books and other similar collections.

Thirdly, JLG has not revised *An Additional Lectionary for use at a Second Sunday Service*, (SPCK and Epworth, 1969). Some churches have adopted this, but it has not been so widely used as JLG 1. Those who wish to have lessons for a second, usually evening, service, could for the most part use two of the lessons of JLG 2, using a year two years distant from the year of the Principal Service.

It is recommended that the use of JLG 2 should begin on the ninth Sunday before Christmas 1992 with Year A.

Raymond George

A Revised Joint Liturgical Group Lectionary

Inclusion of the totality of scripture is not a practical proposition for any conceivable Sunday lectionary scheme. It is clear that the volume of biblical material and the bulk imbalance between Old Testament and New make comprehensive coverage impossible. There is further widespread recognition that not all scripture is liturgically usable. In any event, the congenial soil for continuous reading is the Office rather than the Liturgy.

Given such recognition and within the limitations it imposes, there remain however two principled and coherent approaches to the liturgical reading of scripture. The one is the way of semi-continuous reading, carried through in all three series of lessons (Old Testament, Epistle, and Gospel). The other is the way of calendrical control through the totality of the Christian Year.

Both could muster impressive buttressing argument. Both could claim significant potential pastoral gain. The first would seem to take the canonical shape of scripture seriously. The second would seem to take the round of the Christian Year with a like seriousness. The potential dangers are equally patent. Where calendrical control reigns, there may be peril that lections will be wrested from their context to support some predetermined emphasis, and that the integrity of the Old Testament will be specially set at risk. Conversely, where semi-continuous reading rules, any meaningful interconnection of the three Sunday lections week by week may threaten to fall irrevocably apart.

In its 1967 work, published in *The Calendar and Lectionary*, the Joint Liturgical Group made a directional choice, outlined its rationale, and spelled out its major implications. A quarter of a century later, reassessment is both proper and inevitable. There has been ample time for use and discussion to run their course and render their verdicts. There has been opportunity for alternative lectionary provisions to stake their claims. After considered review, the Joint Liturgical Group reaffirms the fundamental principles on which the 1967 lectionary was based and the controlling approach which characterised it. Modifications in the detailed working out of those principles is another matter. Serious attempt has therefore now been made to deal with identified flaws in previous implementation. Along the way, certain significant questions have had to be faced and answered.

(1) Is the maintenance of calendrical control compatible with any serious representation of semi-continous reading? An affirmative answer can be

returned, provided that the all-important link within each weekly triad of Sunday lections is not menaced. Simultaneous semi-continuous readings in Old Testament, Epistle, and Gospel would destroy such interconnected emphasis. A measure of semi-continuous reading in one biblical strand at a time does not. Such semi-continous selectivity is the true dialogue partner of calendrical control. Within such spacious limits, getting the best of both worlds emerges as a viable proposition.

The integrity of such a harmonising enterprise depends upon decisions and understandings relating to Calendar. The influence and content of this latter can be maximised or minimised. The beating heart of Calendar is Festival; first Easter, secondarily Christmas. Festival then generates Season – a 'Sundays-embracing' extension of Festival that may attract its own 'preparation'. Traditionally, construction has halted at about this point. Within such a perspective, Festival must control its own lections, but Season may lie open to a greater hospitality towards semi-continuous reading of some biblical book judged in general to be suitable. The Easter Season flows at last into Pentecost, which itself ushers in an extended stretch of Ordinary Time. Calendrically, this can be felt to be a wasteland or at least an unfilled interim, till once more Advent dawns. It accordingly offers itself as a native home for further semi-continuous reading of an extended kind.

Such a familiar perception partly arises from an overt and central christological foundation. The Festival Seasons focus and chart the movement of Jesus the Christ from incarnation to ascension, from 'coming' to 'going'. Ordinary Time, especially post-Pentecost, can then appear wholly interim, in so far as it may seem to signal an extended unfocused gap between 'going' and 'coming'. Theologically and liturgically, however, such Ordinary Time remains in the deepest sense Festival Time. The reason for this is that Sunday is the recurrent bedrock on which all else finally rests, the unitive festival of creation and new creation which inherently safeguards Calendar from too narrow a christological concentration (or, worse still, an impoverished 'Jesus' concentration). Each Sunday embodies the fulness of synoptic vision, standing sentinel against the threat that linear historical time be allowed to break loose from its eschatological moorings. The problem of the Christian Year is, from this point of view, an unhealed theological and liturgical incoherence in the relating of Festival Time and Ordinary Time, of 'Season' and 'Sunday'. Lectionary, controlled throughout by an overarching principle and perspective, is one important source of potential coherence.

It is therefore no accident that in 1967 the Joint Liturgical Group sought to present a re-examination and re-presentation of Calendar as providing the inescapable precondition and control for lectionary conclusions. In one sense, the calendrical principles and development put forward were an attempt to impart stronger trinitarian depth to the Christian Year. This was effected by filling the interim hiatus between the christological 'going' and 'coming' with a major pre-Christmas period that moved forward from God's work of creation to the Word made flesh, and with a major post-Pentecost period that focused the presence and work of the Holy Spirit in the life and mission of a Church living between Pentecost and Parousia and on pilgrimage to the ends of the earth and the end of time. In addition, the christological heart of the traditional Calendar was in intention strengthened by a Lenten structure ('The King and the Kingdom'), designed more closely to reflect the costly embattled march to victory of the One who announced and embodied the strange good news and presence of the Kingdom.

(2) Given the maintenance of calendrical control, does a *two year* Sunday lectionary provision still follow? One powerful trend has been to opt for a three year cycle, as represented by the Roman Catholic lectionary and by its modified version, the Common Lectionary. The significant objections to a two year cycle have been that on the one hand it silences the voice of large tracts of scripture and that on the other hand it imposes undue monotony and restrictiveness upon the preaching enterprise. The first charge is arguably more serious than the second. The liturgical reading of scripture is finally to be judged not as a resource for preachers but as a formative declaration to congregations. In any case, it is probably the unwarranted significance given to the indications of thrust attached to each Sunday lectionary provision and an accompanying exaltation of thematic preaching that have heavily promoted the sense of repetitive constriction. Nevertheless, a felt problem is not to be ignored; and any move that may encourage and facilitate the declaration of the whole counsel of God is not to be despised.

In so far as a two year lectionary cycle denies a hearing to the full range of scripture, a more basic issue is indeed at stake. The narrative voice of the Old Testament is likely to be specially muffled. A concealed and unargued canon within the canon is likely to steer the craft of biblical passage selection. It is a partial answer to admit and recognise that any realistically imaginable lectionary will inescapably embody selectivity, that to be aware of the grossest perils should assist damage limitation, and that current halting at a three year cycle testifies to felt limits on liturgically viable scriptural material. Nevertheless, the central point remains.

The Joint Liturgical Group has concluded that an extended cycle is amply warranted, that the limits of such a cycle are currently under-estimated and that, within the limits of liturgically usable biblical material and without serious breaching of the principle of calendrical control, a four year provision is practicable. The fourfoldness of 'Gospel' within the New Testament canon is congruous with this decision and gives added shape to its implementation. A rich coverage of the total New Testament and some enhancement of representation of the narrative material of the Old Testament alike become possible.

(3) Given the maintenance of the fundamental principles of Calendar and Lectionary reform enunciated and reaffirmed, what subsidiary modifications are to be envisaged when lectionary provision is extended from a two year to a four year cycle? Though the links between the three lessons of each individual Sunday remain intentional and strong, the ordered progression through the movement of the Christian Year, hitherto expressed by the presence in so considerable a measure of a *common emphasis* in particular Sunday lectionary provisions *across Year 1 and Year 2*, is inevitably loosened and weakened, and disappears post-Pentecost. Outside the major Festivals, common emphases across four years are no longer a viable option on anything like the former two year scale.

If this means loss for tidy minds, it also signals gain. It can hasten the banishment of preoccupation with 'themes', so homiletically attractive but so widely misunderstood. It further shifts the overt markers of unifying coherence to the points where they controllingly belong – to 'Season' and to 'Sunday'; so that what matters is that the lections on any Sunday should in their measure interrelate and that the lectionary emphases of any group of Sundays should in their measure be seasonally appropriate, congruous with the Festival in whose shadow, closely or remotely, they stand.

This shift means, additionally, that semi-continuous reading can in proper and properly subsidiary fashion find a place and add its strength. Narrative 'Acts' can to a limited extent make its semi-continuous appearance. Given the foundational attachment of a specific Gospel to a specific year, the reading of each distinctive Evangelist can march through the post-Pentecost terrain in more or less continuously ordered fashion. This however does not mean that the Gospel now continues beyond Pentecost as the controlling reading – as if still 'setting the theme'. The language of 'control', like the language of 'theme', may in this connection usefully disappear altogether, provided only that the guiding rubric ensures that, whatever else may be omitted, the Old Testament lesson is always read in the pre-Christmas period, the Gospel always read from Christmas to Ascension, and the Epistle always read in the post-Pentecost period.

Neville Clark

The Lectionary Use of Scripture

In the compilation of the Joint Liturgical Group Lectionary of 1967 due regard was paid to the matter of adequacy of biblical coverage, to the requirement to do justice to the balance of scripture, and to the further need to maintain a proper balance in the various parts of the Liturgy by guarding against lectionary overloading. By all these difficult and elusive concerns the preparation of the revised Lectionary has also, in intention, been governed.

How far execution matches intention, only experience and use will decide. Some facts and figures, however, may in a preliminary way assist judgement. From the Pentateuch, 672 different verses have been used, with particular emphasis on Genesis (274), on Exodus (229), and on Deuteronomy (108). The Historical Books, Joshua to 2 Chronicles, have provided 514 verses. From the Major Prophets, 599 verses have been culled: 364 from Isaiah, 146 from Jeremiah, 89 from Ezekiel. The Minor Prophets, from Hosea to Malachi, have yielded 170 verses. From the remaining books of the Old Testament, 283 verses have been pressed into service. The total material deployed from the Old Testament therefore amounts to *2238* verses. This compares with 991 used by the original Lectionary.

Material provided from the Four Gospels is substantial and totals *2718* verses. From Matthew, 643 verses are drawn; from Mark, 514; from Luke, 737, from John 824. This total provision of 2718 verses compares with 1338 in the 1967 Lectionary.

The remaining books of the New Testament yielded 1073 verses in the original Lectionary. The revised Lectionary has used *2136*. Of these: 412 are from Acts; 1204 from the 'Pauline' Letters (including, Romans: 284; 1 Corinthians: 233; 2 Corinthians: 133; Ephesians: 143); 159 from Hebrews; 272 from the other New Testament Letters; 89 from the Revelation.

The overall use of scripture amounts therefore to *7092* different verses, 2238 coming from the Old Testament, and 4854 from the New Testament.

Duplication of lections, while inevitable, has been kept to a minimum. The overwhelming majority of cases (some 850 verses) arise when and because a Sunday lection also demands attachment to Christmas Day, Epiphany, Ash Wednesday, Maundy Thursday, Good Friday, Ascension Day, *or* because of traditional practice in connection with Palm Sunday, *or* as a result of the inalienable claim of the great Festival Sundays upon a particular scriptural passage year by year. In a few additional cases, the sense of a passage or the integrity of a reading has demanded minor lectionary overlap. For the rest, about 90 verses straightforwardly reoccur in more than one year because of intrinsic importance or suitability.

In a minority of instances, some bracketted provision has been made for chosen lections to be extended. Some suggestions have also been made where it is desired to observe Mothering Sunday.

The issue of lectionary overloading allows of no simple solution, and constantly calls for delicate and difficult judgements which must have one eye on the ideal and one eye on the practicable. In 1967, a guideline of thirty verses was adopted. That conclusion has been reaffirmed. In the event, the average revised Lectionary provision remains the same, hovering between the two poles of 30 and 31 – nearer the first in Years A and B, nearer the second in years C and D. It is in a minority of cases only that a set of lections amounts to more than forty verses. Five of these are in Year A, 5 in Year B, 7 in Year C, 6 in Year D.

Neville Clark

Index

to Joint Liturgical Group Four Year Lectionary

NOTES

1. Passages marked by an asterisk are cases where a choice is offered. Please refer to the lectionary for each occasion.

2. The Sunday or Feast is marked by a code: the letter refers to the season
   C for Christmas
   Ep for Epiphany
   L for Lent — Easter i = First Easter Day Service
   E for Easter — Easter ii = Second Easter Day Service
   P for Pentecost;
   the number precedes or follows the letter to signify the place of the Sunday in its season
   9C means 9th Sunday *before* Christmas
   E12 means 12th Sunday *after* Easter

Lection	*Sunday*	*Year*
Genesis		
1.1–5, 24–31a	9C	D
1.1–5, 26–31	Easter i	A*
2.4b–9, 15–25	9C	B
3.1–15	8C	D
3.8–13, 22–24	Easter i	B*
4.1–10	8C	B
6.5–8	P20	C
6.11–22	5E(L2)	C
7.1–5, 10–18;		
8.6–18		
9.8–13	Easter i	C*
8.15–22	Harvest	A
9.8–17	8C	C
11.1–9	Pentecost	C
12.1–9	7C	D
13.1–18	7C	A
14.18–20	Maundy	C
15.1–18	7C	B
17.1–10	P21	C
18.1–16	7C	C
18.23–33	E5	B
21.(1–8) 9–21	P8	A
21.8–21	Mothering	*
22.1–18	Palm	D*
	GdFri	B
24.62–67	P12	A
25.29–34	2E (L5)	A
28.10–22	Ep4	A
32.22–32	P18	B
37.(2–11) 12–28	P16	C
41.1–7, 25–32	Harvest	C
45.1–15	P16	A
Exodus		
2.1–10	6C	D
2.11–22	P21	B
3.1–15	6C	C
4.27 — 5.1	Easter i	D*
6.2–13	6C	B
12.1–8, 11–14	Maundy	B
12.21–27	P17	B
13.17–22	P14	D
14.15–22	Ep1	B
	Easter i	ABCD
14.15 — 15.1	Easter i	ABCD*
15.1–11	E1	D
16.4–15	E3	C
17.3–7	6E(L1)	D
18.13–27	Ep2	C
19.1–6	E4	B
19.3–8, 16–20	P1	C
20.1–17	AshWed	D
	P17	A

Lection	*Sunday*	*Year*
20.8–11	Ep6	C
22.21–27	P10	C
23.10–13	P13	C
24.3–8	Maundy	A
24.3–11	3E(L4)	A
24.12–18	3E(L4)	B
32.7–14	P19	B
33.7–11	E5	D
33.12–23	Ep3	D
34.4–9	P13	D
34.29–35	3E(L4)	C
Leviticus		
19.9–18	E3	B
	Harvest	D*
25.15–22	Harvest	B
25.39–46	P19	C
Numbers		
9.15–23	Ep3	C
11.24–29	P9	B
13.1–2, 17–33	E1	B
27.15–23	P22	C
Deuteronomy		
4.1–8	P20	A
5.12–15	Ep6	D
6.4–9	P1	B
6.10–17	6E(L1)	C
6.17–25	P2	D
7.6–11	E4	C
8.1–6	7E	D
8.11–20	P3	C
10.12 — 11.1	P10	B
15.1–11	P16	B
18.15–22	6C	A
26.1–11	P4	A
	Harvest	D*
30.11–15	Ep3	B
30.15–20	6E(L1)	A
31.22–29	Easter i	D*
Joshua		
1.1–9	Pentecost	B
2.1–14	P8	C
3.1–17	Ep1	C
6.1–20	P19	A
24.14–24	4E(L3)	D
Judges		
6.36–40	P11	D
7.1–8, 19–23	PLast	C

Lection	*Sunday*	*Year*
9.7–15	Ep5	D
11.29–40	P21	D
13.2–14	2C(A3)	A
Ruth		
1.1–18 (19–22)	P5	C
1 Samuel		
1.9–20	Mothering	*
1.20–28	C2	C
2.1–10	1C(A4)	B
3.1–10	Ep2	D
9.27 — 10.1, 6–7	3E(L4)	D
16.1–13	5C	B
16.1–13a	Ep1	A
16.14–23	P3	B
17.(32–37) 38–50	P8	B
21.1–6	Ep6	A
24.7b–17	P7	C
2 Samuel		
1.17–27	E4	A
5.1–5	5C	C
7.4–16	P2	C
12.1–13a	Ep5	B
16.1–13	P22	B
18.(24–30) 31–33	P15	C
23.13–17	P22	D
1 Kings		
3.4–15	P14	A
8.22–30	Ep4	D
10.1–13	P7	B
17.8–16	P9	D
17.(8–16) 17–24	E2	A
18.20–39	E5	A
19.(1–8) 9–21	P9	C
21.1–16	P15	B
22.(1–5) 6–17	3C(A2)	D
2 Kings		
2.1–15	E6	D
4.18–37	8E	B
5.1–14 (15–19a)	8E	A
6.8–17	5E(L2)	D
7.1–16	E1	C
1 Chronicles		
29.(1–5) 6–19	Ep4	B
2 Chronicles		
6.12–21	P6	A
7.11–16	P17	D

Lection	Sunday	Year
15.1–8	P2	B
Nehemiah		
2.1–18	E3	A
6.1–16	P21	A
Esther		
4.10 — 5.8	P5	B
Job		
1.1–12	4E(L3)	A
2.1–10	8E	C
22.12–28	9E	D
23.1–10	8E	D
28.12–28	P12	D
38.1–18	9C	C
42.1–6	P20	D
Proverbs		
2.1–9	9E	B
3.1–8	9E	C
3.13–20	P18	D
8.1, 22–31	9C	A
9.1–11	P10	D
25.2–7	P14	C
Ecclesiastes		
3.1–13	P18	A
Isaiah		
1.10–17	Ep6	B
2.1–5	4C(A1)	A
5.1–7	P13	B
6.1–8	P1	A
6.(1–7) 8–12	Ep5	A
7.10–14	1C(A4)	A
	ChrMid	D
9.1–4	Ep3	A
9.2, 6–7	ChrMid	B
	Christmas	A
11.1–10	1C(A4)	C
	C1	D
12.1–6	Easter ii	A
25.1–9	PLast	B
30.8–17	7E	A
30.18–21	9E	A
33.17–22	PLast	A
35.1–10	5E(L2)	A
40.1–11	2C(A3)	B
40.12–17	P1	D
40.25–31	C2	D
41.8–16	7E	C

Lection	Sunday	Year
42.1–9	Ep1	D
42.10–16	Easter ii	B
43.1–13	P8	D
44.6–17	8C	A
45.1–7	E6	B
45.14–25	P22	A
45.22–25	ChrMid	C
48.1–8	4E(L3)	B
49.1–6	Ep	B
49.7–13	C1	B
	Ep	D
49.13–23	Ep	A
49.14–21	P5	A
50.4–7	Palm	B*
50.4–9	GdFri	D
51.1–6	E2	C
51.4–11	4C(A1)	B
52.1–10	4C(A1)	D
52.7–14	Christmas	B
52.13 — 53.12	GdFri	C
54.1–8	P11	B
54.4–14	Easter i	C*
55.1–11	3C(A2)	C
	Easter i	B*
	Easter ii	D
56.1–8	Palm	C*
58.1–8	AshWed	B*
59.12–20	3C(A2)	A
60.1–6	C1	A
	Ep	C
60.19–22	P3	A
61.1–3	E2	D
61.1–11	C1	C
62.1–5	E3	D
62.6–7, 10–12	Christmas	D
63.1–9	2E(L5)	D
63.7–14	4E(L3)	C
65.17–25	E1	A
66.5–13	Mothering	*
Jeremiah		
1.4–10	Ep2	B
2.1–13	5E(L2)	B
7.1–7	P7	A
10.1–10a	E6	A
13.1–11	Ep5	C
20.7–13	P11	A
23.1–6	5C	D
23.23–32	P6	B
28.1–17	P15	D
29.1, 4–14	PLast	D
31.1–6	Easter ii	C

Lection	Sunday	Year
31.15–17	C2	A
31.15–20	Mothering	*
31.27–34	6E(L1)	B
31.31–34	Maundy	D
33.14–16	4C(A1)	C
36.1–10	3C(A2)	B
38.1–13	P6	C
50.4–7	P16	D
Lamentations		
1.1–14	2E(L5)	C
2.15–19	GdFri	A
3.(1–9) 18–33	2E(L5)	B
5.15–22	Palm	A*
Ezekiel		
2.1 — 3.4	Ep2	A
12.21–28	P11	C
18.25–32	P2	A
34.1–6	P4	C
34.7–15	E2	B
36.16–28	Easter i	A*
36.24–28	E4	D
37.1–14	Pentecost	D
37.15a–28	P15	A
43.1–7a	E6	C
Daniel		
3.13–26	P20	B
6.10–23	E5	C
7.13–14	AscDay	ABCD
12.1–4	P19	D
Hosea		
6.1–6	P9	A
11.1–9	P14	B
14.1–7	P6	D
Joel		
2.12–18	AshWed	A
2.23–29	Pentecost	A
Amos		
5.6–15	AshWed	C
5.18–24	P12	C
6.1–7	P18	C
7.10–15	P4	B
8.4–7	P17	C
Jonah		
1.1–17	7E	B
3.1–5	P10	A

Lection	Sunday	Year
(3.6–10) 4.1–11	P5	D
Micah		
2.12–13	5C	A
4.1–7	P4	D
5.2–4	ChrMid	A
	Christmas	C
6.1–8	P12	B
7.14–20	P7	D
Habakkuk		
2.1–4	P3	D
3.17–19	P13	A
Zephaniah		
3.14–18	2C(A3)	C
Haggai		
2.1–9	Ep4	C
Zechariah		
2.10–13	1C(A4)	D
8.1–8	C2	B
9.9 (–10)	Palm	ABCD*
Malachi		
4.1–6	2C(A3)	D
Matthew		
1.18–23	1C(A4)	A
2.1–12	C1	ABCD*
	Ep	ABCD
2.13–23	C2	A
3.1–6	P2	A
3.7–12	7C	A
3.13–17	Ep1	A
4.1–11	6E(L1)	AD
4.12–17	Ep3	A
4.18–25	Ep2	A
5.1–12	PLast	B
5.(1–12) 17–20	9E	A
5.13–16	P3	A
5.21–37	P4	A
5.38–48	6C	A
6.1–15	AshWed	D
	E5	A
6.16–21	AshWed	A
6.22–34	P5	A
6.25–34	Harvest	A
7.1–14	P6	A

Lection	*Sunday*	*Year*
7.15–29	P7	A
8.5–13	P8	A
9.9–13	P9	A
9.35 — 10.16	P10	A
10.16–25	P11	A
10.28–33	9C	A
11.2–19	2C(A3)	A
11.25–30	P1	A
12.1–14	Ep6	A
12.14–21	Pentecost	A
12.22–32	5E(L2)	A
12.38–42	E2	A
12.43–50	P12	A
13.10–17	Ep5	A
13.24–43	P13	A
13.44–52	P14	A
13.53–58	3C(A2)	A
14.22–36	7E	A
15.21–31	8E	A
16.13–28	4E(L3)	A
17.1–13	3E(L4)	A
18.10–20	P15	A
18.21–35	P16	A
19.13–30	P17	A
20.1–16	P18	A
20.20–28	2E(L5)	A
21.1–11	Palm	A*
21.12–16	Ep4	A
21.18–32	P19	A
22.15–22	P20	A
23.25–36	8C	A
23.29–39	Mothering	*
24.36–44	4C(A1)	A
25.1–13	PLast	A
25.14–30	P21	A
25.31–46	5C	A
26.6–13	P22	A
26.26–35	Maundy	A
(26.36 — 27.31)	{ Palm	AD*
27.32–54 (55–56)	{ GdFri	A*
28.1–10	Easter i	AD
28.11–15	E1	A
28.16–20	AscDay	A
	E6	C

Mark

Lection	*Sunday*	*Year*
1.1–8	2C(A3)	B
1.9–11	Ep1	B
	P1	B
1.12–15	6E(L1)	B
1.14–20	Ep2	B
1.21–28	Ep3	B
1.29–39	P2	B
1.40–45	Ep4	B
2.1–12	8E	B
2.18–22	AshWed	B
2.23 — 3.6	Ep6	B
3.19b–27	5E(L2)	B
3.19b–30	Pentecost	B*
3.31–35	Mothering	*
4.1–9	9E	B
4.1–9, 13–20	Harvest	B
4.10–12, 21–34	Ep5	B
4.26–34	Pentecost	B*
4.35–41	7E	B
5.1–20	P3	B
6.1–13	P4	B
6.14–29	P5	B
7.1–13	3C(A2)	B
7.14–23	8C	B
8.14–21	P6	B
8.22–26	P7	B
8.27–33	4E(L3)	B
8.31 — 9.1	AscDay	B*
9.2–10	3E(L4)	B
9.14–29	P8	B
9.33–41	P9	B
9.42–50	P10	B
10.2–12	9C	B
10.13–16	P11	B
10.17–31	5C	B
10.32–45	2E(L5)	B
10.46–52	P12	B
11.1–11	Palm	B*
12.1–12	P13	B
12.18–27	7C	B
12.28–34	P14	B
12.35–44	P15	B
13.5–13	6C	B
13.21–37	4C(A1)	B
14.1–9	P16	B
14.10–25	P17	B
14.12–26	Maundy	B
14.26–42	P18	B
14.43–52	P19	B
14.53–65	P20	B
14.66–72	P21	B
15.1–21	P22	B
(14.32 — 15.20)	{ Palm	B*
15.21–39 (40–41)	{ GdFri	B*
16.1–8	Easter i	B
16.15–20	AscDay	B*

Lection	Sunday	Year
Luke		
1.5–25	2C(A3)	C
1.26–38a	1C(A4)	C
1.39–45 (46–55)	Mothering	*
1.39–56	1C(A4)	B
1.57–66	1C(A4)	D
2.1–20	ChrMid	ABD
	Christmas	C
2.21–40	C2	C
2.41–52	C2	B
	Mothering	*
3.1–14	7C	C
3.15–22	Ep1	C
4.1–13	6E(L1)	C
4.14–21	3C(A2)	C
4.16–30	Ep3	C
5.1–11	Ep2	C
5.12–26	8E	C
5.33–39	Ep5	C
6.1–11	Ep6	C
7.1–10	E5	C
7.11–17	P6	C
7.36–50	P7	C
8.1–3	P8	C
8.4–15	9E	C
8.40–56	P3	C
9.10–17	7E	C
9.18–27	4E(L3)	C
9.28–36	3E(L4)	C
9.51–62	P9	C
10.17–24	P1	C
10.25–42	P10	C
11.1–13	Pentecost	C
11.14–26	5E(L2)	C
11.33–41	8C	C
12.13–31	9C	C
12.16–31	Harvest	C
12.35–48	P11	C
13. (1–9) 10–17	P12	C
14.1–6	P13	C
14.7–14	P14	C
14.15–24	P2	C
14.25–35	P15	C
15.1–10	P4	C
15.11–32	P16	C
16.1–13	P17	C
16.19–31	P18	C
17.1–10	P19	C
17.11–19	P5	C
17.20–37	P20	C
18.1–14	AshWed	C
19.1–10	P21	C
19.11–27	PLast	C
19.29–40 (41–44)	Palm	C*
20.1–8	P22	C
20.9–19	2E(L5)	C
20.27–40	6C	C
21.1–9	Ep4	C
21.25–36	4C(A1)	C
22.14–38	Maundy	C
(22.39 — 23.31)	{ Palm	C*
23.32–49	{ GdFri	C
23.35–43	5C	C
24.1–11	Easter i	C
24.13–35	E1	C
24.36–43	E2	C
24.44–53	AscDay	C
	E6	A
John		
1.1–14	9C	D
	ChrMid	C
	Christmas	ABD
1.14–18	C2	D
1.19–28	2C(A3)	D
1.29–34	Ep1	D
1.35–51	Ep2	D
2.1–11	Ep3	D
2.13–25	Ep4	D
3.1–15	P2	D
3.13–21	8C	D
3.22–36	P3	D
4.5–26	P4	D
4.27–42	P5	D
4.43–54	P6	D
5.1–18	8E	D
5.19–36	P7	D
5.36–47	3C(A2)	D
6.1–15	7E	D
6.16–21	P8	D
6.22–27	P9	D
6.27–35	6C	D
6.35–40	E3	C
6.41–59	P10	D
6.60–71	4E(L3)	D
7.1–17	P11	D
7.14–24	Ep6	D
7.25–31	4C(A1)	D
7.32–39	E6	D
7.40–52	P12	D
8.3–11	P13	D
8.12–20	P14	D
8.21–36	9E	D

Lection	*Sunday*	*Year*
8.(31–36) 37–47	P15	D
8.51–59	7C	D
9.(1–12) 13–41	5E(L2)	D
10.1–6	P16	D
10.7–18	E2	B
10.22–30	P17	D
10.31–42	P18	D
11.1–16	P19	D
11.17–27	E3	A
11.28–44	P20	D
11.45–54	P21	D
12.1–8	3E(L4)	D
12.12–16	Palm	D*
12.20–36	2E(L5)	D
12.23–28	Harvest	D
12.37–50	Ep5	D
13.1–15	Maundy	D
13.12–30	P22	D
13.31–35	E3	B
14.1–11	E4	A
14.8–17	P1	D
14.15–27	Pentecost	D
15.1–11	E4	B
15.12–17	E4	C
15.18–27	E4	D
16.1–11	AscDay	D
16.12–24	E5	B
16.25–33	E5	D
17.1–13	E6	B
17.13–26	PLast	D
18.1–40	Palm	D*
18.1 — 19.37	GdFri	ABCD*
18.33–40	5C	D
20.1–18	Easter ii	ABCD
20.19–31	E1	BD
21.1–14	E2	D
21.15–25	E3	D

Acts

Lection	*Sunday*	*Year*
1.1–11	AscDay	ABCD
1.12–26	E6	C
2.1–11	Pentecost	ABCD
2.(14–21) 22–36	P1	C
2.37–47	P2	C
3.1–10	8E	C
3.11–26	6C	A
4.5–12	P3	C
4.13–31	P2	B
4.32–37	P5	A
5.27–42	P20	B
6.1–7	P22	D
7.44–50	Ep4	A
7.54 — 8.1	P22	B
8.5–8, 14–17	P22	C
8.26–38	P4	C
9.1–20	Ep2	B
9.26–31	P10	A
9.36–43	P6	D
10.34–48a	Ep1	C
11.4–18	P5	C
12.1–17	7E	A
13.1–12	P4	B
13.13–25	P5	B
13.26–31	E1	A
13.44–52	P13	B
14.8–17	9C	C
15.1–2, 22–29	P22	A
16.(6–10) 11–15	Ep2	C
16.16–24	P3	B
17.22–34	P2	A
19.13–20	P7	A
20.7–12	P6	C
20.17–35	P11	A
24.10–21	P7	D
27.33–44	P8	D
28.1–6	7E	C

Romans

Lection	*Sunday*	*Year*
1.1–7	1C(A4)	B
1.8–17	Ep3	A
1.18–25	Ep5	A
2.1–11	Ep6	A
3.21–28	8C	A
4.1–12	P21	C
4.13–25	7C	D
5.1–11	2E(L5)	B
5.12–21	8C	C
6.3–11	Easter i	ABCD
6.12–23	Ep1	A
7.1–6	P13	D
7.7–13	8C	D
8.1–11	2E(L5)	A
8.12–17	P1	B
8.18–25	P13	A
8.22–27	E5	B
8.28–39	E5	D
9.1–9	7C	C
9.19–28	P8	A
10.5–17	P2	D
10.8–13	6E(L1)	C
11.13–24	4C(A1)	D
11.33–36	P18	D
12.1–8	C2	C
12.9–21	P10	C

Lection	*Sunday*	*Year*
13.1–10	P20	A
13.8–14	4C(A1)	A
14.1–9	P13	C
14.10–23	P9	D
15.4–13	3C(A2)	C
15.13–21	Ep	A
16.1–7	Mothering	*
16.25–27	3C(A2)	A

1 Corinthians

Lection	*Sunday*	*Year*
1.1–9	Ep3	C
1.10–17	P15	A
1.18–25	Palm	A*
1.26–31	1C(A4)	C
2.1–5	Ep5	C
2.6–10	9E	B
2.11 — 3.9	P12	D
3.10–17	Ep4	D
3.18–23	Ep6	C
4.1–5	2C(A3)	D
4.8–16	9E	C
5.7b–8	Easter ii	D
6.12–20	Ep4	B
8.1–13	E3	C
9.19–27	AshWed	B
10.1–13	Ep5	D
10.16–17	Maundy	AC
11.23–29	Maundy	BD
	P10	D
12.3–13	E3	A
12.14–26	P9	B
12.27 — 13.13	P14	B
15.1–11	Easter ii	B
15.12–20	Easter ii	C
15.20–28	5C	C
15.35–52	P14	A
15.50–58	E2	C

2 Corinthians

Lection	*Sunday*	*Year*
1.3–11	C2	A
1.15–22	3E(L4)	D
2.14 — 3.6	Ep6	D
3.4–18	3E(L4)	C
4.1–6	3E(L4)	B
4.7–18	E1	B
5.1–10	P19	D
5.14 — 6.2	AshWed	D
	P9	A
6.1–10	P8	B
6.14 — 7.1	Ep4	C
8.1–15	P4	A
9.6–15	P16	B
	Harvest	D
11.7–15	P14	C
12.1–10	8E	A

Galatians

Lection	*Sunday*	*Year*
1.1–10	P15	B
1.11–24	Ep2	D
2.11–21	4E(L3)	D
3.1–14	7C	A
3.23 — 4.7	E4	C
3.26 — 4.7	C1	D
4.1–7	Ep	B
4.21 — 5.1	Mothering	*
5.2–11	P6	B
5.13–25	E4	D
6.1–10	P7	C
6.7–10	Harvest	A
6.14–18	P15	C

Ephesians

Lection	*Sunday*	*Year*
1.3–14	P1	A
1.15–23	E6	B
2.1–10	Ep1	D
2.11–22	P5	D
3.1–12	C1	A
	Ep	C
3.14–21	P17	D
4.1–16	E6	A
4.17–32	P12	B
5.1–5	P17	A
5.6–14	5E(L2)	D
5.11–20	P14	D
5.21 — 6.4	P11	B
6.10–20	5E(L2)	B

Philippians

Lection	*Sunday*	*Year*
1.1–11	P20	C
1.12–30	P20	D
2.1–13	ChrMid	C
2.5–11	Palm	B*
2.12–18	P3	A
3.7–21	PLast	D
4.1–3	P8	C
4.4–9	2C(A3)	A
4.10–20	7E	D
	Harvest	B

Colossians

Lection	*Sunday*	*Year*
1.1–14	C2	D
1.15–20	9C	D
1.18–23	GdFri	D
1.21–29	P18	B

Lection	*Sunday*	*Year*
2.8–15	2E(L5)	D
2.16–19	Ep6	B
3.1–11	E2	A
3.12–17	P16	C
3.18 — 4.1	P12	A
1 Thessalonians		
1.1–10	P11	C
2.1–8	C2	B
	Mothering	*
5.1–11	4C(A1)	B
5.16–24	2C(A3)	C
2 Thessalonians		
3.1–5	E5	C
3.6–13	P18	A
1 Timothy		
1.12–17	5C	B
2.1–8	P6	A
3.14–16	P7	B
4.(4–7a) 7b–16	9E	A
6.1–12	P17	C
6.11–16	P1	D
2 Timothy		
1.8–14	4E(L3)	B
2.1–7	AshWed	A
2.8–13	4E(L3)	C
3.14 — 4.8	3C(A2)	B
Titus		
2.11–15	ChrMid	A
	Christmas	C
3.4–7	ChrMid	B
	Christmas	D
Philemon		
1–25	P19	C
Hebrews		
1.1–6	ChrMid	D
	Christmas	B
2.1–4	7E	B
2.10–18	6E(L1)	B
3.1–6	6C	D
4.12–16	6E(L1)	D
4.14–16; 5.7–9	GdFri	B
5.1–10	2E(L5)	C
6.4–9	P19	B
7.11–25 (26–28)	E5	A
8.1–13	6C	C

Lection	*Sunday*	*Year*
9.11–15 (16–22)	P21	D
9.23–28	P17	B
10.1–10	1C(A4)	D
	Palm	C*
10.11–25	Palm	D*
	GdFri	AC
11.1–2, 11–12	Mothering	*
11.17–22, 29–31	P19	A
11.17–29	6C	B
11.23–28	P21	B
11.32 — 12.2	PLast	C
12.3–13	P10	B
12.18–29	P4	D
James		
1.2–5	8E	D
1.12–18	6E(L1)	A
1.19–27	P12	C
2.1–9	P18	C
2.8–13	P16	A
2.14–26	7C	B
4.1–10	AshWed	C
5.1–11	4C(A1)	C
5.13–16	8E	B
1 Peter		
1.3–9	E1	D
1.3–12	Ep3	B
1.13–25	E2	D
1.22–25	Ep5	B
2.1–10	E4	B
2.11–25	P16	D
3.13–22	P9	C
4.7–11	P21	A
4.12–19	4E(L3)	A
5.1–11	E2	B
2 Peter		
1.16–19	3E(L4)	A
1.19 — 2.3	3C(A2)	D
3.8–14	2C(A3)	B
1 John		
1.1–4	Ep3	D
1.1 — 2.2	C1	C
2.1–11	E4	A
2.22–29	P3	D
3.1–10	5E(L2)	A
3.9–18	8C	B
4.1–6	5E(L2)	C
4.7–14	Christmas	A
4.13–21	E3	B

Lection	Sunday	Year
5.1–5	P11	D
5.6–9	Ep1	B
5.10–21	P15	D

2 John

Lection	Sunday	Year
1–13	9E	D

Revelation

Lection	Sunday	Year
1.4–8	5C	D
1.12–18	Easter ii	A
3.14–22	E3	D
4.1–11	9C	B
5.6–14	E6	D
7.2–4, 9–12	PLast	B
7.9–17	PLast	A
10.8–11	Ep2	A
11.19 — 12.6	1C(A4)	A
14.14–18	Harvest	C
19.6–9	E1	C
19.11–16	5C	A
21.1–4, 22–27	9C	A
21.22 — 22.5	C1	B
	Ep	D

A Four Year Lectionary

It is best to read all the lessons, but if any are omitted, the Old Testament should always be read on Sundays before Christmas, the Gospel from Christmas Day to the 6th Sunday after Easter (the Sun after Ascension Day) and the Epistle or equivalent New Testament lesson from Pentecost to the I Sunday after Pentecost. Verses in brackets may be omitted.

SUNDAY OR HOLY DAY	YEAR A	YEAR B	YEAR C	YEAR D
9th Sunday before Christmas	Prov. 8. 1, 22–31 Rev. 21. 1–4, 22–27 Matt. 10. 28–33	Gen. 2. 4b–9, 15–25 Rev. 4. 1–11 Mark 10. 2–12	Job 38. 1–18 Acts 14. 8–17 Luke 12. 13–31	Gen. 1. 1–5, 24–31a Col. 1. 15–20 John 1. 1–14
8th Sunday before Christmas	Isa. 44. 6–17 Rom. 3. 21–28 Matt. 23. 25–36	Gen. 4. 1–10 1 John 3. 9–18 Mark 7. 14–23	Gen. 9. 8–17 Rom. 5. 12–21 Luke 11. 33–41	Gen. 3. 1–15 Rom. 7. 7–13 John 3. 13–21
7th Sunday before Christmas	Gen. 13. 1–18 Gal. 3. 1–14 Matt. 3. 7–12	Gen. 15. 1–18 Jas. 2. 14–26 Mark 12. 18–27	Gen. 18. 1–16 Rom. 9. 1–9 Luke 3. 1–14	Gen. 12. 1–9 Rom. 4. 13–25 John 8. 51–59
6th Sunday before Christmas	Deut. 18. 15–22 Acts 3. 11–26 Matt. 5. 38–48	Exod. 6. 2–13 Heb. 11. 17–29 Mark 13. 5–13	Exod. 3. 1–15 Heb. 8. 1–13 Luke 20. 27–40	Exod. 2. 1–10 Heb. 3. 1–6 John 6. 27–35
5th Sunday before Christmas	Micah 2. 12–13 Rev. 19. 11–16 Matt. 25. 31–46	1 Sam. 16. 1–13 1 Tim. 1. 12–17 Mark 10. 17–31	2 Sam. 5. 1–5 1 Cor. 15. 20–28 Luke 23. 35–43	Jer. 23. 1–6 Rev. 1. 4–8 John 18. 33–40
4th Sunday before Christmas (Advent 1)	Isa. 2. 1–5 Rom. 13. 8–14 Matt. 24. 36–44	Isa. 51. 4–11 1 Thess. 5. 1–11 Mark 13. 21–37	Jer. 33. 14–16 Jas. 5. 1–11 Luke 21. 25–36	Isa. 52. 1–10 Rom. 11. 13–2 John. 7. 25–31
3rd Sunday before Christmas (Advent 2)	Isa. 59. 12–20 Rom. 16. 25–27 Matt. 13. 53–58	Jer. 36. 1–10 2 Tim. 3.14 — 4.8 Mark 7. 1–13	Isa. 55. 1–11 Rom. 15. 4–13 Luke 4. 14–21	1 Kings 22. (1– 6–17 2 Pet. 1.19 — 2 John 5. 36–47
2nd Sunday before Christmas (Advent 3)	Judg. 13. 2–14 Phil 4. 4–9 Matt. 11. 2–19	Isa. 40. 1–11 2 Pet. 3. 8–14 Mark 1. 1–8	Zeph. 3. 14–18 1 Thess. 5. 16–24 Luke 1. 5–25	Mal. 4. 1–6 1 Cor. 4. 1–5 John 1. 19–28

H 160 15.12.96 P. 13.12.98 AM H. 13.12.98 P

NDAY OR HOLY DAY	YEAR A	YEAR B	YEAR C	YEAR D
nday next before Christmas (Advent 4)	Isa. 7. 10–14 Rev. 11.19 — 12.6 Matt. 1. 18–23	1 Sam. 2. 1–10 Rom. 1. 1–7 Luke 1. 39–56	Isa. 11. 1–10 1 Cor. 1. 26–31 Luke 1. 26–38a	Zech. 2. 10–13 Heb. 10. 1–10 Luke 1. 57–66
	Lk. 1. 68–79 may well be used as a canticle.		H. 22.12.96	
ristmas (midnight)	Micah 5. 2–4 Titus 2. 11–15 Luke 2. 1–20	Isa. 9. 2, 6–7 Titus 3. 4–7 Luke 2. 1–20	Isa. 45. 22–25 Phil. 2. 1–13 John 1. 1–14	Isa. 7. 10–14 Heb. 1. 1–6 Luke 2. 1–20
ristmas Day	Isa. 9. 2, 6–7 1 John 4. 7–14 John 1. 1–14	Isa. 52. 7–14 Heb. 1. 1–6 John 1. 1–14	Micah 5. 2–4 Titus 2. 11–15 Luke 2. 1–20	Isa. 62. 6–7, 10–12 Titus 3. 4–7 John 1. 1–14
Sunday after Christmas	Isa. 60. 1–6 Eph. 3. 1–12 Matt. 2. 1–12	Isa. 49. 7–13 Rev. 21. 22 — 22.5 Matt. 2. 1–12	Isa. 61. 1–11 1 John 1.1 — 2.2 Matt. 2. 1–12	Isa. 11. 1–10 Gal. 3. 26–4:7 Matt. 2. 1–12
	When this day falls on December 30th, the lessons of the 2nd Sunday after Christmas are read.			
d Sunday after Christmas	Jer. 31. 15–17 2 Cor. 1. 3–11 Matt. 2. 13–23	Zech. 8. 1–8 1 Thess. 2. 1–8 Luke 2. 41–52	1 Sam. 1. 20–28 Rom. 12. 1–8 Luke 2. 21–40	Isa. 40. 25–31 Col. 1. 1–14 John 1. 14–18
iphany	Isa. 49. 13–23 Rom. 15. 13–21 Matt. 2. 1–12	Isa. 49. 1–6 Gal. 4. 1–7 Matt. 2. 1–12	Isa. 60. 1–6 Eph. 3. 1–12 Matt. 2. 1–12	Isa. 49. 7–13 Rev. 21.22 — 22.5 Matt. 2. 1–12
Sunday after Epiphany	1 Sam. 16. 1–13a Rom. 6. 12–23 Matt. 3. 13–17 P. 12.01.97	Exod. 14. 15–22 1 John 5. 6–9 Mark 1. 9–11	Josh. 3. 1–17 Acts 10. 34–48a Luke 3. 15–22	Isa. 42. 1–9 Eph. 2. 1–10 John 1. 29–34
d Sunday after Epiphany	Ezek. 2. 1 — 3.4 Rev. 10. 8–11 Matt. 4. 18–25	Jer. 1. 4–10 Acts 9. 1–20 Mark 1. 14–20	Exod. 18. 13–27 Acts 16. (6–10) 11–15 Luke 5. 1–11	1 Sam. 3. 1–10 Gal. 1. 11–24 John 1. 35–51
d Sunday after Epiphany	Isa. 9. 1–4 Rom. 1. 8–17 Matt. 4. 12–17 H. 26.01.97 (PM)	Deut. 30. 11–15 1 Pet. 1. 3–12 Mark 1. 21–28 P. 26.01.97 (AM)	Num. 9. 15–23 1 Cor. 1. 1–9 Luke 4. 16–30	Exod. 33. 12–23 1 John 1. 1–4 John 2. 1–11
n Sunday after Epiphany	Gen. 28. 10–22 Acts 7. 44–50 Matt. 21. 12–16 H. 2.02.97 (AM)	1 Chr. 29. (1–5) 6–19 1 Cor. 6. 12–20 Mark 1. 40–45 H. 1.02.98 (AM)	Hagg. 2. 1–9 2 Cor. 6.14 — 7.1 Luke 21. 1–9	1 Kings 8. 22–30 1 Cor. 3. 10–17 John 2. 13–25
h Sunday after Epiphany	Isa. 6. (1–7) 8–12 Rom. 1. 18–25 Matt. 13. 10–17 H 9.02.97. (PM)	2 Sam 12. 1–13a 1 Pet. 1. 22–25 Mark 4. 10–12, 21–34 P. 9.02.97 AM	Jer. 13. 1–11 1 Cor. 2. 1–5 Luke 5. 33–39	Judg. 9. 7–15 1 Cor. 10. 1–13 John 12. 37–50

SUNDAY OR HOLY DAY	YEAR A	YEAR B	YEAR C	YEAR D
6th Sunday after Epiphany	1 Sam. 21. 1–6 Rom. 2. 1–11 Matt. 12. 1–14	Isa. 1. 10–17 Col. 2. 16–19 Mark 2.23 — 3.6	Exod. 20. 8–11 1 Cor. 3. 18–23 Luke 6. 1–11	Deut. 5. 12–15 2 Cor. 2.14 — 3 John 7. 14–24
9th Sunday before Easter	Isa. 30. 18–21 1 Tim. 4. (4–7a) 7b–16 Matt. 5. (1–12) 17–20	Prov. 2. 1–9 1 Cor. 2. 6–10 Mark 4. 1–9	Prov. 3. 1–8 1 Cor. 4. 8–16 Luke 8. 4–15	Job 22. 12–28 2 John 1–13 John 8. 21–36
8th Sunday before Easter	2 Kings 5. 1–14 (15–19a) 2 Cor. 12. 1–10 Matt. 15. 21–31	2 Kings 4. 18–37 Jas. 5. 13–16 Mark 2. 1–12	Job 2. 1–10 Acts 3. 1–10 Luke 5. 12–26	Job 23. 1–10 Jas. 1. 2–5 John 5. 1–18
7th Sunday before Easter	Isa. 30. 8–17 Acts 12. 1–17 Matt. 14. 22–36	Jonah 1. 1–17 Heb. 2. 1–4 Mark 4. 35–41	Isa. 41. 8–16 Acts 28. 1–6 Luke 9. 10–17	Deut. 8: 1–6 Phil. 4. 10–20 John 6. 1–15
Ash Wednesday	Joel 2. 12–18 2 Tim. 2. 1–7 Matt. 6. 16–21	Isa. 58. 1–8 1 Cor. 9. 19–27 Mark 2. 18–22	Amos 5. 6–15 Jas. 4. 1–10 Luke 18. 1–14	Exod. 20. 1–17 2 Cor. 5.14 — 6 Matt. 6. 1–15
6th Sunday before Easter (Lent 1)	Deut. 30. 15–20 Jas. 1. 12–18 Matt. 4. 1–11	Jer. 31. 27–34 Heb. 2. 10–18 Mark 1. 12–15	Deut. 6. 10–17 Rom. 10. 8–13 Luke 4. 1–13	Exod. 17. 3–7 Heb. 4. 12–16 Matt. 4. 1–11
5th Sunday before Easter (Lent 2)	Isa. 35. 1–10 1 John 3. 1–10 Matt. 12. 22–32	Jer. 2. 1–13 Eph. 6. 10–20 Mark 3. 19b–27	Gen. 6. 11–22 1 John 4. 1–6 Luke 11. 14–26	2 Kings 6. 8–17 Eph. 5. 6–14 John 9. (1–12) 13–41
4th Sunday before Easter (Lent 3)	Job 1. 1–12 1 Pet. 4. 12–19 Matt. 16. 13–28	Isa. 48. 1–8 2 Tim. 1. 8–14 Mark 8. 27–33	Isa. 63. 7–14 2 Tim. 2. 8–13 Luke 9. 18–27	Josh. 24. 14–24 Gal. 2. 11–21 John 6. 60–71
3rd Sunday before Easter (Lent 4)	Exod. 24. 3–11 2 Pet. 1. 16–19 Matt. 17. 1–13	Exod. 24: 12–18 2 Cor. 4. 1–6 Mark 9. 2–10	Exod. 34. 29–35 2 Cor. 3. 4–18 Luke 9. 28–36	1 Sam 9.27 — 10.1, 6–7 2 Cor. 1. 15–22 John 12. 1–8
	These lessons are appropriate also for the Sunday nearest to August 6th.			
Mothering Sunday	Isa. 66. 5–13; *or* Jer. 31. 15–20; *or* Gen. 21. 8–21; *or* 1 Sam. 1. 9–20 Rom. 16. 1–7; *or* 1 Thess. 2. 1–8; *or* Gal. 4. 21 — 5.1; *or* Heb. 11. 1–2, 11–12 Matt. 23. 29–39; *or* Mark 3. 31–35; *or* Luke 1. 39–45 (46–55); *or* Luke 2. 41–52			
2nd Sunday before Easter (Lent 5)	Gen. 25. 29–34 Rom. 8. 1–11 Matt. 20. 20–28	Lam. 3. (1–9) 18–33 Rom. 5. 1–11 Mark 10. 32–45	Lam. 1. 1–14 Heb. 5. 1–10 Luke 20. 9–19	Isa. 63. 1–9 Col. 2. 8–15 John 12. 20–36

NDAY OR HOLY DAY	YEAR A	YEAR B	YEAR C	YEAR D
m Sunday	Zech. 9. 9 (10) Matt. 21. 1–11	Zech. 9. 9 (10) Mark 11. 1–11	Zech. 9. 9 (10) Luke 19. 29–40 (41–44)	Zech. 9. 9 (10) John 12. 12–16
	-----------------	-----------------	-----------------	-----------------
	Lam. 5. 15–22 1 Cor. 1. 18–25 Matt. (26.36 — 27.31) 27. 32–54 (55–56)	Isa. 50. 4–7 Phil. 2. 5–11 Mark (14.32 — 15.20) 15. 21–39 (40–41)	Isa. 56. 1–8 Heb. 10. 1–10 Luke (22. 39 — 23.31) 23. 32–49	Gen. 22. 1–18 Heb. 10. 11–25 Matt. (26. 36 — 27.31) 27. 32–54 (55–56) *or* John 18. 1–40
	On this day and on Good Friday provision is made, as is traditional for reading the greater part of the passion narratives, but where these passages are not read in full, the earlier parts of the narratives may be read at evening services during Lent or on the Monday, Tuesday and Wednesday of Holy Week.			
undy Thursday	Exod. 24. 3–8 1 Cor. 10. 16–17 Matt. 26. 26–35	Exod. 12. 1–8, 11–14 1 Cor. 11. 23–29 Mark 14. 12–26	Gen. 14. 18–20 1 Cor. 10. 16–17 Luke 22. 14–38	Jer. 31. 31–34 1 Cor. 11. 23–29 John 13. 1–15
od Friday	Lam. 2. 15–19 Heb. 10. 11–25 John (18.1 — 19.16) 19. 17–37 *or* Matt. (26.36 — 27.31) 27. 32–54 (55–56)	Gen. 22. 1–18 Heb. 4. 14–16; 5. 7–9 John (18.1 — 19.16) 19. 17–37 *or* Mark (14.32 — 15.20) 15. 21–39 (40–41)	Isa. 52.13 — 53.12 Heb. 10. 11–25 John (18.1 — 19.16) 19. 17–37 *or* Luke (22.39 — 23.31) 23. 32–49	Isa. 50. 4–9 Col. 1. 18–23 John (18.1 — 19.16) 19. 17–37 *or* John 18.1 — 19.37 *or* John 19. 1–37 *or* John 19. 17–37
ster Day (first service)	(Gen. 1. 1–5, 26–31) Exod. 14.15–22 *or* 14.15 — 15.1 (Ezek. 36. 16–28) Rom. 6. 3–11 Matt. 28. 1–10	(Gen. 3. 8–13, 22–24) Exod. 14.15–22 *or* 14.15 — 15.1 (Isa. 55. 1–11) Rom. 6. 3–11 Mark 16. 1–8	(Gen. 7.2–5, 10–18, 8.6–18; 9.8–13) Exod. 14.15–22 *or* 14.15 — 15.1 (Isa. 54. 4–14) Rom. 6. 3–11 Luke 24. 1–11	(Exod. 4.27 — 5.1) Exod. 14.15–22 *or* 14.15 — 15.1 (Deut. 31. 22–29) Rom. 6. 3–11 Matt. 28. 1–10
	If the service includes a vigil, all the lessons should be read. If it is in the early morning. those in brackets should be omitted.			
(second service)	Isa. 12. 1–6 Rev. 1. 12–18 John 20. 1–18	Isa. 42. 10–16 1 Cor. 15. 1–11 John 20. 1–18	Jer. 31. 1–6 1 Cor. 15. 12–20 John 20. 1–18	Isa. 55. 1–11 1 Cor. 5. 7b–8 John 20. 1–18
Sunday after Easter	Isa. 65. 17–25 Acts 13. 26–31 Matt. 28. 11–15	Num. 13. 1–2, 17–33 2 Cor. 4. 7–18 John 20. 19–31	2 Kings 7. 1–16 Rev. 19. 6–9 Luke 24. 13–35	Exod. 15. 1–11 1 Pet. 1. 3–9 John 20. 19–31

H. 6.4.97(AM) H. 6.4.97(PM)

SUNDAY OR HOLY DAY	YEAR A	YEAR B	YEAR C	YEAR D
2nd Sunday after Easter	1 Kings 17. (8–16) 17–24 Col. 3. 1–11 Matt. 12. 38–42	Ezek. 34. 7–15 1 Pet. 5. 1–11 John 10. 7–18	Isa. 51. 1–6 1 Cor. 15. 50–58 Luke 24. 36–43	Isa. 61. 1–3 1 Pet. 1. 13–25 John 21. 1–14
3rd Sunday after Easter	Neh. 2. 1–18 1 Cor. 12. 3–13 John 11. 17–27	Lev. 19. 9–18 1 John 4.13–21 John 13. 31–35	Exod. 16. 4–15 1 Cor. 8. 1–13 John 6.35–40	Isa. 62. 1–5 Rev. 3. 14–22 John 21. 15–25
4th Sunday after Easter	2 Sam. 1. 17–27 1 John 2. 1–11 John 14. 1–11	Exod. 19. 1–6 1 Pet. 2. 1–10 John 15. 1–11	Deut. 7. 6–11 Gal. 3.23 — 4.7 John 15. 12–17	Ezek. 36. 24–28 Gal. 5. 13–25 John 15. 18–27
5th Sunday after Easter	1 Kings 18. 20–39 Heb. 7. 11–25 (26–28) Matt. 6. 1–15	Gen. 18. 23–33 Rom. 8. 22–27 John 16. 12–24	Dan. 6. 10–23 2 Thess. 3. 1–5 Luke 7. 1–10	Exod. 33. 7–11 Rom. 8. 28–39 John 16. 25–33
Ascension Day	Dan. 7. 13–14 Acts 1. 1–11 Matt. 28. 16–20	Dan. 7. 13–14 Acts 1. 1–11 Mark 16. 15–20 *or* Mark 8.31 — 9.1	Dan. 7. 13–14 Acts 1. 1–11 Luke 24. 44–53	Dan. 7. 13–14 Acts 1. 1–11 John 16. 1–11
6th Sunday after Easter (Sunday after Ascension Day)	Jer. 10. 1–10a Eph. 4. 1–16 Luke 24. 44–53	Isa. 45. 1–7 Eph. 1. 15–23 John 17. 1–13	Ezek. 43. 1–7a Acts 1. 12–26 Matt. 28. 16–20	2 Kings 2. 1–15 Rev. 5. 6–14 John 7. 32–39
Pentecost	Joel 2. 23–29 Acts 2. 1–11 Matt. 12. 14–21	Josh. 1. 1–9 Acts 2. 1–11 Mark 4. 26–34 *or* Mark 3. 19b–30	Gen. 11. 1–9 Acts 2. 1–11 Luke 11. 1–13	Ezek. 37. 1–14 Acts 2. 1–11 John 14. 15–27
1st Sunday after Pentecost (Trinity Sunday)	Isa. 6. 1–8 Eph. 1. 3–14 Matt. 11. 25–30	Deut. 6. 4–9 Rom. 8. 12–17 Mark 1. 9–11	Exod. 19. 3–8, 16–20 Acts 2. (14–21) 22–36 Luke 10. 17–24	Isa. 40. 12–17 1 Tim. 6. 11–16 John 14. 8–17
2nd Sunday after Pentecost	Ezek. 18. 25–32 Acts 17. 22–34 Matt. 3. 1–6	2 Chron. 15. 1–8 Acts 4. 13–31 Mark 1. 29–39	2 Sam. 7. 4–16 Acts 2. 37–47 Luke 14. 15–24	Deut. 6. 17–25 Rom. 10. 5–17 John 3. 1–15
3rd Sunday after Pentecost	Isa. 60. 19–22 Phil. 2. 12–18 Matt. 5. 13–16	1 Sam. 16. 14–23 Acts 16. 16–24 Mark 5. 1–20	Deut. 8. 11–20 Acts. 4.5–12 Luke 8. 40–56	Hab. 2. 1–4 1 John 2. 22–29 John 3. 22–36

NDAY OR HOLY DAY	YEAR A	YEAR B	YEAR C	YEAR D
Sunday after Pentecost	Deut. 26. 1–11 2 Cor. 8. 1–15 Matt. 5. 21–37	Amos 7. 10–15 Acts 13. 1–12 Mark 6. 1–13	Ezek. 34. 1–6 Acts 8. 26–38 Luke 15. 1–10	Micah 4. 1–7 Heb. 12. 18–29 John 4. 5–26
Sunday after Pentecost	Isa. 49. 14–21 Acts 4. 32–37 Matt. 6. 22–34	Esther 4.10 — 5.8 Acts 13. 13–25 Mark 6. 14–29	Ruth 1. 1–18 (19–22) Acts 11. 4–18 Luke 17. 11–19	Jonah (3. 6–10) 4. 1–11 Eph. 2. 11–22 John 4. 27–42
Sunday after Pentecost	2 Chron. 6. 12–21 1 Tim. 2. 1–8 Matt. 7. 1–14	Jer. 23. 23–32 Gal. 5. 2–11 Mark 8. 14–21	Jer. 38. 1–13 Acts 20. 7–12 Luke 7. 11–17	Hos. 14. 1–7 Acts 9. 36–43 John 4. 43–54
Sunday after Pentecost	Jer. 7. 1–7 Acts 19. 13–20 Matt. 7. 15–29	1 Kings 10. 1–13 1 Tim. 3. 14–16 Mark 8. 22–26	1 Sam. 24. 7b–17 Gal. 6. 1–10 Luke 7. 36–50	Micah 7. 14–20 Acts 24. 10–21 John 5. 19–36
Sunday after Pentecost	Gen. 21. (1–8) 9–21 Rom. 9. 19–28 Matt. 8. 5–13	1 Sam. 17. (32–37) 38–50 2 Cor. 6. 1–10 Mark 9. 14–29	Josh. 2. 1–14 Phil. 4. 1–3 Luke 8. 1–3	Isa. 43. 1–13 Acts 27. 33–44 John 6. 16–21
Sunday after Pentecost	Hos. 6. 1–6 2 Cor. 5.14 — 6.2 Matt. 9.9–13	Num. 11. 24–29 1 Cor. 12. 14–26 Mark 9. 33–41	1 Kings 19. (1–8) 9–21 1 Pet. 3. 13–22 Luke 9. 51–62	1 Kings 17. 8–16 Rom. 14. 10–23 John 6. 22–27
n Sunday after Pentecost	Jonah 3. 1–5 Acts 9. 26–31 Matt. 9.35 — 10.16	Deut. 10.12 — 11.1 Heb. 12. 3–13 Mark 9. 42–50	Exod. 22. 21–27 Rom. 12. 9–21 Luke 10. 25–42	Prov. 9. 1–11 1 Cor. 11. 23–29 John 6. 41–59
n Sunday after Pentecost	Jer. 20. 7–13 Acts. 20. 17–35 Matt. 10. 16–25	Isa. 54. 1–8 Eph. 5.21 — 6.4 Mark 10. 13–16	Ezek. 12. 21–28 1 Thess. 1. 1–10 Luke 12. 35–48	Judg. 6. 36–40 1 John 5. 1–5 John 7. 1–17
Sunday after Pentecost	Gen. 24. 62–67 Col. 3.18 — 4.1 Matt. 12. 43–50	Micah 6. 1–8 Eph. 4. 17–32 Mark 10. 46–52	Amos 5. 18–24 Jas. 1. 19–27 Luke 13. (1–9) 10–17	Job 28. 12–28 1 Cor. 2.11 — 3.9 John 7.40–52
Sunday after Pentecost	Hab. 3. 17–19 Rom. 8. 18–25 Matt. 13. 24–43	Isa. 5. 1–7 Acts 13. 44–52 Mark 12. 1–12	Exod. 23. 10–13 Rom. 14. 1–9 Luke 14. 1–6	Exod. 34. 4–9 Rom. 7. 1–6 John 8. 3–11
Sunday after Pentecost	1 Kings 3. 4–15 1 Cor. 15. 35–52 Matt. 13. 44–52	Hos. 11. 1–9 1 Cor. 12.27 — 13.13 Mark 12. 28–34	Prov. 25. 2–7 2 Cor. 11. 7–15 Luke 14. 7–14	Exod. 13. 17–22 Eph. 5. 11–20 John 8. 12–20

SUNDAY OR HOLY DAY	YEAR A	YEAR B	YEAR C	YEAR D
15th Sunday after Pentecost	Ezek. 37. 15a–28 1 Cor. 1. 10–17 Matt. 18. 10–20	1 Kings 21. 1–16 Gal. 1. 1–10 Mark 12. 35–44	2 Sam. 18. (24–30) 31–33 Gal. 6. 14–18 Luke 14. 25–35	Jer. 28. 1–17 1 John 5. 10–21 John 8 (31–36) 37–47
16th Sunday after Pentecost	Gen. 45. 1–15 Jas. 2. 8–13 Matt. 18. 21–35	Deut. 15. 1–11 2 Cor. 9. 6–15 Mark 14. 1–9	Gen. 37. (2–11) 12–28 Col. 3. 12–17 Luke 15. 11–32	Jer. 50. 4–7 1 Pet. 2. 11–25 John 10. 1–6
17th Sunday after Pentecost	Exod. 20. 1–17 Eph. 5. 1–5 Matt. 19. 13–30	Exod. 12. 21–27 Heb. 9. 23–28 Mark 14. 10–25	Amos 8. 4–7 1 Tim. 6 1–12 Luke 16. 1–13	2 Chron. 7. 11–1 Eph. 3. 14–21 John 10. 22–30
18th Sunday after Pentecost	Eccles. 3. 1–13 2 Thess. 3. 6–13 Matt. 20. 1–16	Gen. 32. 22–32 Col. 1. 21–29 Mark 14. 26–42	Amos 6. 1–7 Jas. 2. 1–9 Luke 16. 19–31	Prov. 3. 13–20 Rom. 11. 33–36 John 10. 31–42
19th Sunday after Pentecost	Josh 6. 1–20 Heb. 11. 17–22, 29–31 Matt. 21. 18–32	Exod. 32. 7–14 Heb. 6. 4–9 Mark 14. 43–52	Lev. 25. 39–46 Philem. 1–25 Luke 17. 1–10	Dan. 12. 1–4 2 Cor. 5. 1–10 John 11. 1–16
20th Sunday after Pentecost	Deut. 4. 1–8 Rom. 13. 1–10 Matt. 22. 15–22	Dan. 3. 13–26 Acts 5. 27–42 Mark 14. 53–65	Gen. 6. 5–8 Phil. 1. 1–11 Luke 17. 20–37	Job 42. 1–6 Phil. 1. 12–30 John 11. 28–44
21st Sunday after Pentecost	Neh. 6. 1–16 1 Pet. 4. 7–11 Matt. 25. 14–30	Exod. 2. 11–22 Heb. 11. 23–28 Mark 14. 66–72	Gen. 17. 1–10 Rom. 4. 1–12 Luke 19. 1–10	Judg. 11. 29–40 Heb. 9. 11–15 (16–22) John 11. 45–54
22nd Sunday after Pentecost	Isa. 45. 14–25 Acts 15. 1–2, 22–29 Matt. 26. 6–13	2 Sam. 16. 1–13 Acts 7.54 — 8.1 Mark 15. 1–21	Num. 27. 15–23 Acts. 8. 5–8, 14–17 Luke 20. 1–8	2 Sam. 23. 13–1 Acts 6. 1–7 John 13. 12–30
Last Sunday after Pentecost	Isa. 33. 17–22 Rev. 7. 9–17 Matt. 25. 1–13	Isa. 25. 1–9 Rev. 7. 2–4, 9–12 Matt. 5. 1–12	Judg. 7. 1–8, 19–23 Heb. 11.32 — 12.2 Luke 19. 11–27	Jer. 29. 1, 4–14 Phil. 3. 7–21 John 17. 13–26
Harvest Festival	Gen. 8. 15–22 Gal. 6. 7–10 Matt. 6. 25–34	Lev. 25. 15–22 Phil. 4. 10–20 Mark 4. 1–9, 13–20	Gen. 41. 1–7, 25–32 Rev. 14. 14–18 Luke 12. 16–31	Deut. 26. 1–11 *or* Lev. 19. 9–18 2 Cor. 9. 6–15 John 12. 23–28